THE STORY OF WORDS

A LOOK AT WRITING THROUGH HISTORY

written by Golriz Golkar
illustrated by Narges Mohammadi

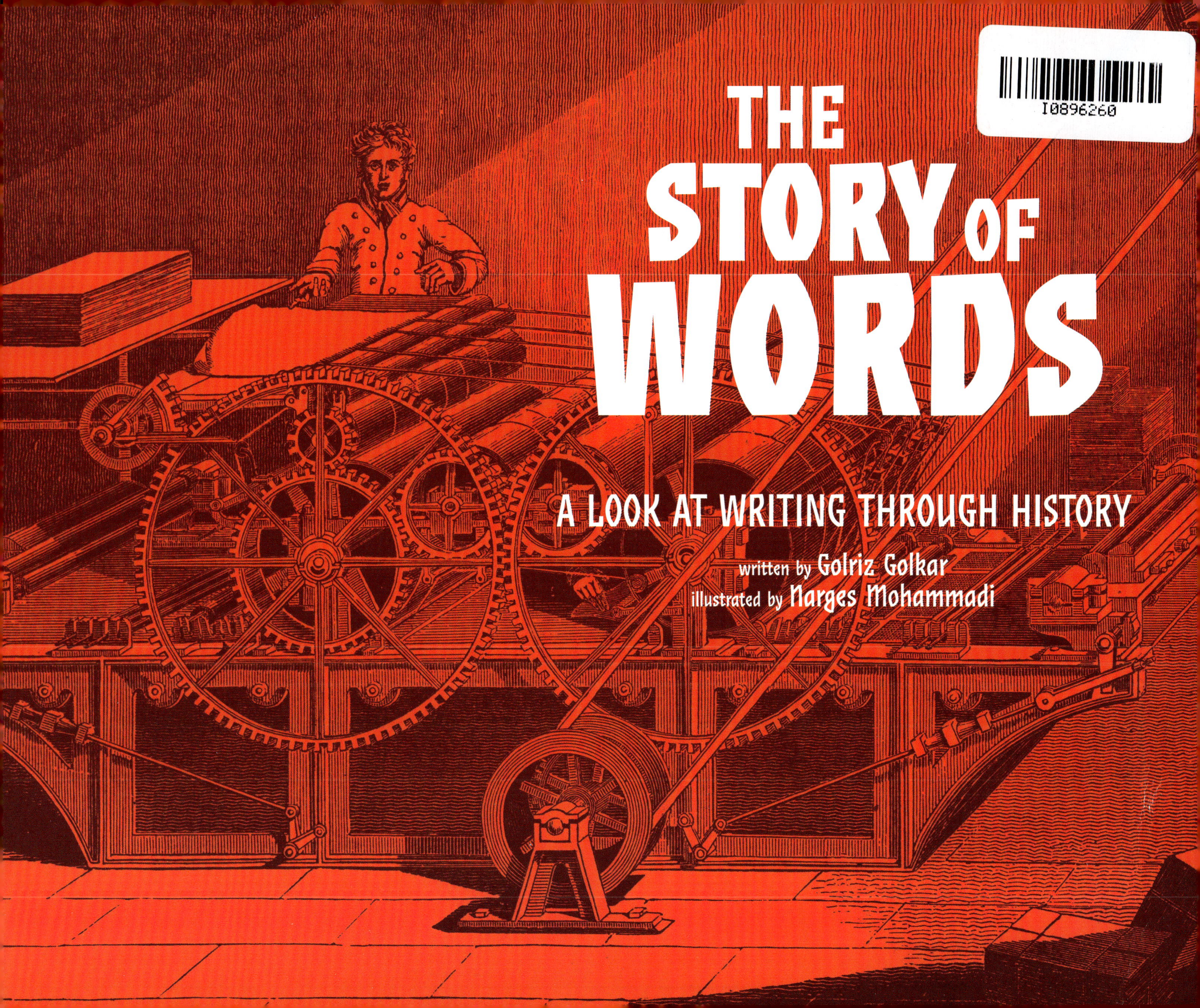

HOW DO WE SHARE IDEAS?

Long ago, people often shared their thoughts by talking to each other. Older people passed down information and stories by telling them to younger people. This helped preserve the history of communities. In many places, these traditions still live on.

But at one point, many people began to write down ideas too. Writing could be saved and read for a long time. And as inventors created new technology, written words could be sent to people far away. Let's take a look at some of the ways people have used writing over the years.

ABOUT 30,000 YEARS AGO

CAVE PAINTINGS

Early people painted pictures of horses, lions, deer, bears, and other animals on cave walls. They used ground-up rocks and burnt wood to make the colors.

Writing didn't exist yet. But experts say cave paintings may have been a way for people to share stories and information. Ancient cave paintings have been found all over the world.

STORIES IN PICTURES

Scientists think that some cave paintings probably told legends and stories. Other pictures may have passed down knowledge about hunting.

Early people were hunters who knew a lot about animals. On some of the paintings they made, you can see lines and dots next to the animals. These marks may have been made to communicate information about each animal, such as where to find it or what time of year to hunt it.

ABOUT 5,500 YEARS AGO

CUNEIFORM WRITING

Cave paintings were followed by writing systems. A writing system shows the words of a language. It can be a pattern of lines, dots, or other shapes. Take a look at the letters and words in this sentence—that's a writing system!

The first known writing system was called cuneiform (kyoo-NEE-ih-form). The people who invented it lived in an area in Asia that was then called Mesopotamia. Today, this area is made up of Iraq and parts of other nearby countries.

Ancient Mesopotamians didn't write on paper. They pressed a stick into a slab of damp clay and let the clay dry into a hard tablet. The symbols stood for words and numbers.

People wrote down notes, laws, and stories. Kids wrote in cuneiform too! They used clay tablets to write their schoolwork. Some of this writing has lasted for thousands of years.

ABOUT 5,100 YEARS AGO

HIEROGLYPHICS

Ancient Egyptians created the next known writing system. This system, called hieroglyphics (hy-ruh-GLIH-fiks), had hundreds of symbols. The symbols included animals like birds and snakes, people, objects, and shapes.

One way that people used hieroglyphics was by carving them onto stone. Many of these carvings still survive on ancient walls and monuments.

Some of the symbols in hieroglyphics stood for words or ideas. Others stood for sounds. Sometimes the same symbol could stand for more than one thing. For example, a picture of a mouth could mean "mouth," or it could stand for the sound of the letter R. That made reading hieroglyphics difficult.

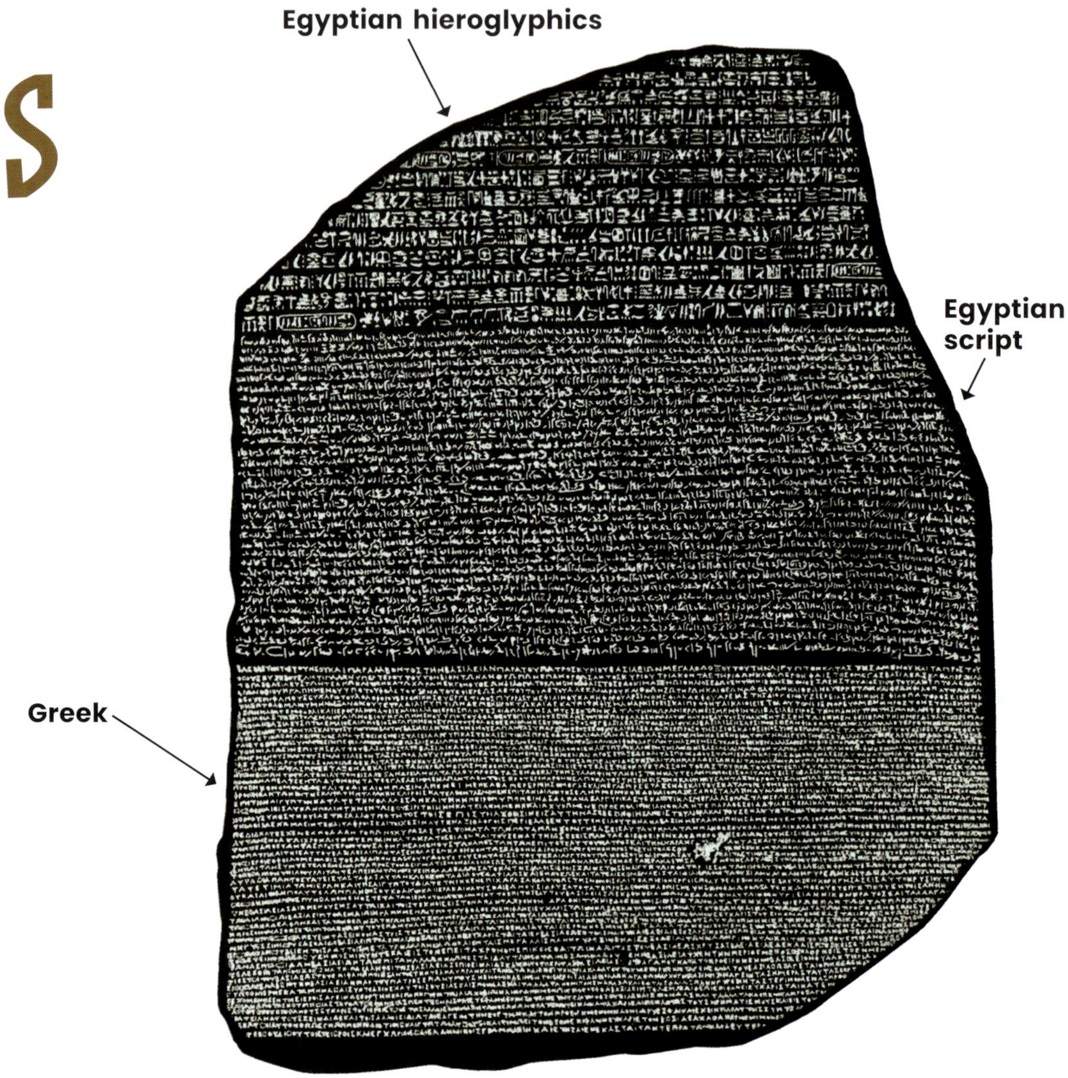

The Rosetta Stone

After people stopped using hieroglyphics, no one remembered how to read them. Then a large, smooth slab of rock was found. Called the Rosetta Stone, it had the same text carved in hieroglyphics and two other writing systems. It helped people figure out how to read hieroglyphics again.

TRY IT YOURSELF!

READ HIEROGLYPHICS

WHAT TO DO

Find the pictures below on the sound symbols chart at right. Write the letter that goes with each picture on the blank above it to spell the answer to a riddle.

What did the ancient Egyptian kid say when he stubbed his toe?

Answer:

SOME SOUND SYMBOLS IN HIEROGLYPHICS

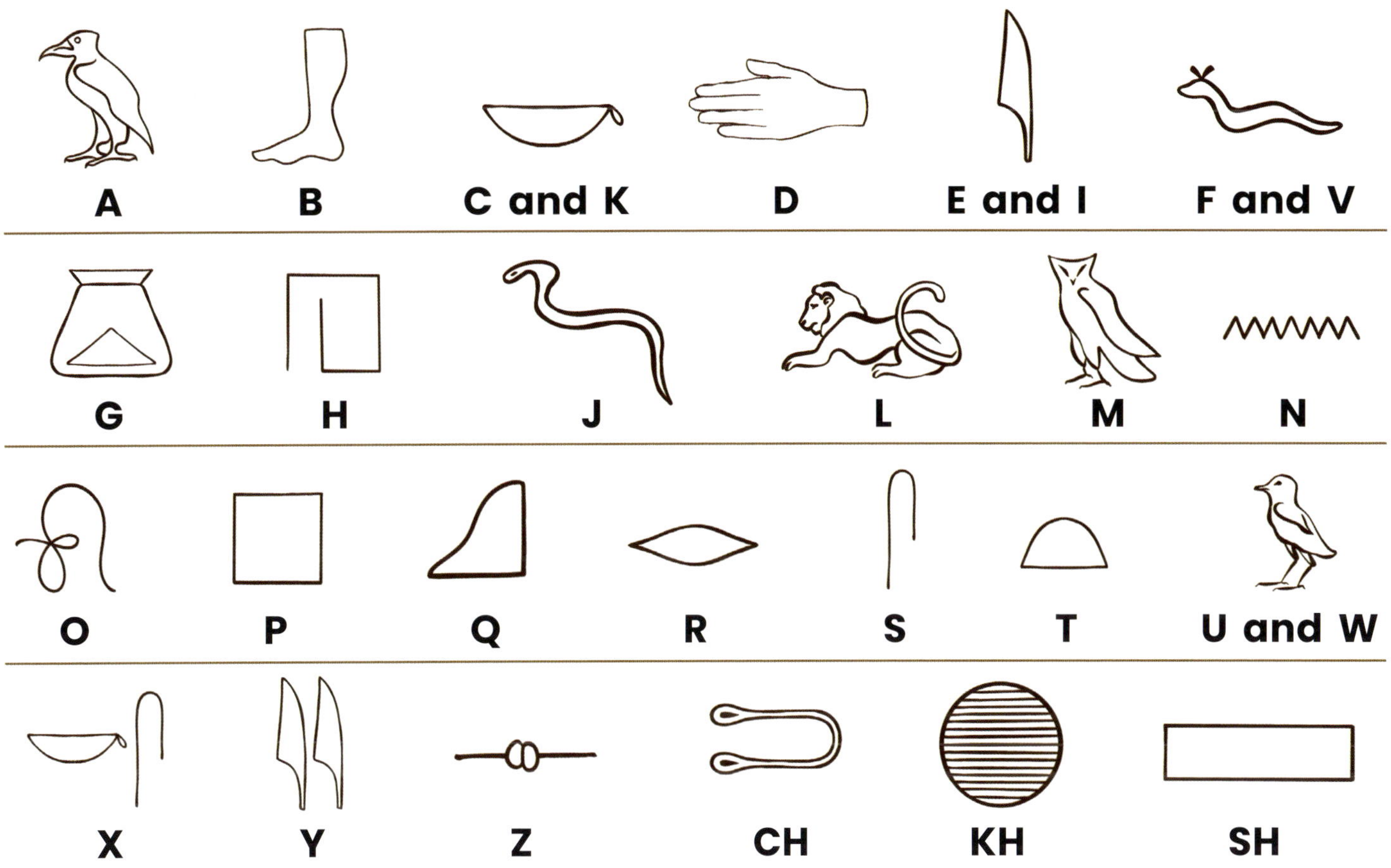

Some sounds that are similar in English, like "f" and "v," are represented by the same symbol in hieroglyphics. If you see one of these symbols as you decode the answer to the riddle, try each letter to see which one makes sense.

ABOUT 5,000 YEARS AGO

PAPYRUS

Egyptian people invented something new that was useful to write on—papyrus. To make it, they cut strips from papyrus plant stems and soaked the strips in water. Then they arranged the strips in layers, hammered them into a flat sheet, and let the papyrus dry. Pieces of papyrus were glued together to make one long sheet that was rolled onto sticks. This was called a scroll.

Ancient Egyptians also invented the first pens! They made them from the hollow stems of plants called reeds. First they carved a reed to make a point. Then they dipped the reed into ink to write on a scroll.

▲ Egyptians wrote in hieroglyphics on papyrus scrolls like this one.

▶ Papyrus plants are tall. They grow in or near water like the Nile River in Egypt.

TRY IT YOURSELF!

MAKE YOUR OWN PAPER

People wrote on papyrus for thousands of years. Today, we write on paper, which is similar. Here's how you can make your own recycled paper.

WHAT YOU NEED

scrap paper

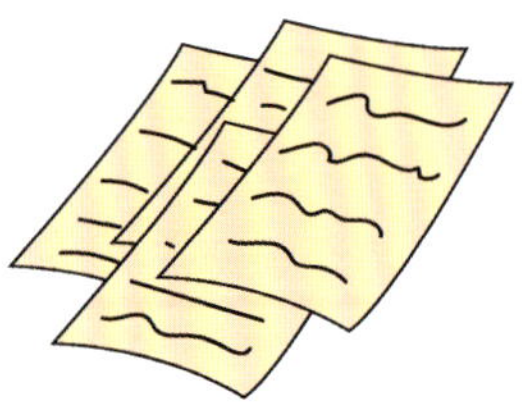

water

blender

fine-mesh strainer

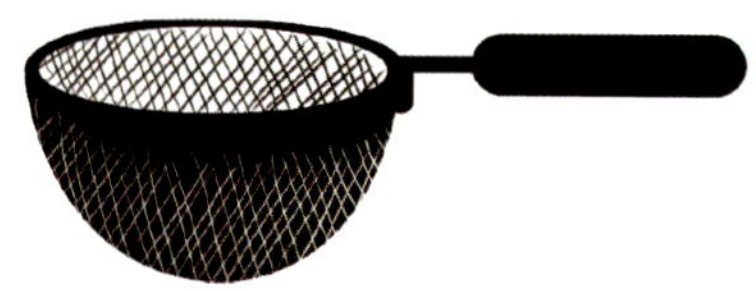

nonstick sheet pan

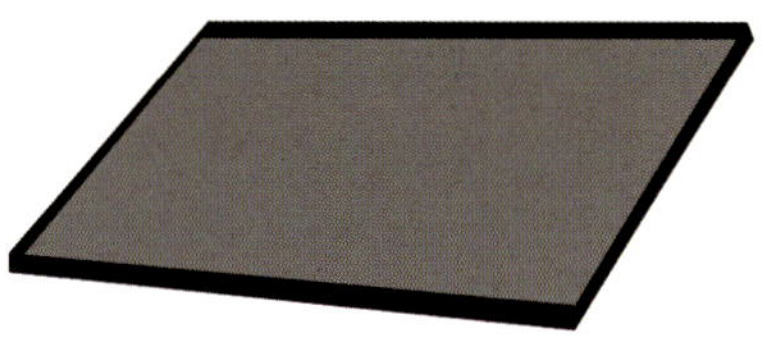

spoon

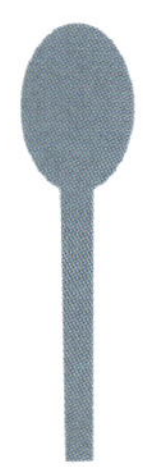

spatula

food coloring (optional)

WHAT TO DO

1

To make one sheet of recycled paper, add two cups of finely ripped or shredded paper and three cups of water to the blender. Let it soak for two hours.

2

Ask an adult to help you turn on the blender and blend it until you have an oatmeal-like mixture. If the mixture gets too thick to blend, add more water.

3

If you like, add some food coloring and blend until it is mixed in.

4

Slowly pour the mixture into the mesh strainer. Let the water drain out until you have wet pulp.

5

Spoon the wet pulp onto the sheet pan. Evenly spread out the pulp and pat it down to make it flat and about 1/3 cm (1/8 inch) thick.

6

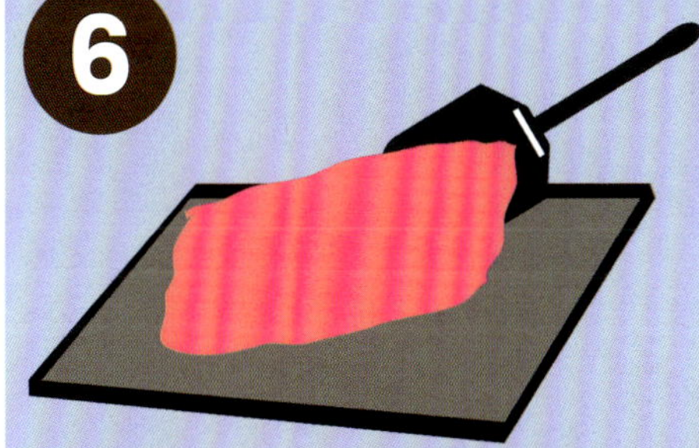

Let the pulp dry completely, about one to two days. (If you put the sheet pan in a warm spot, it will dry faster.) Use the spatula to carefully lift your recycled paper off the sheet pan.

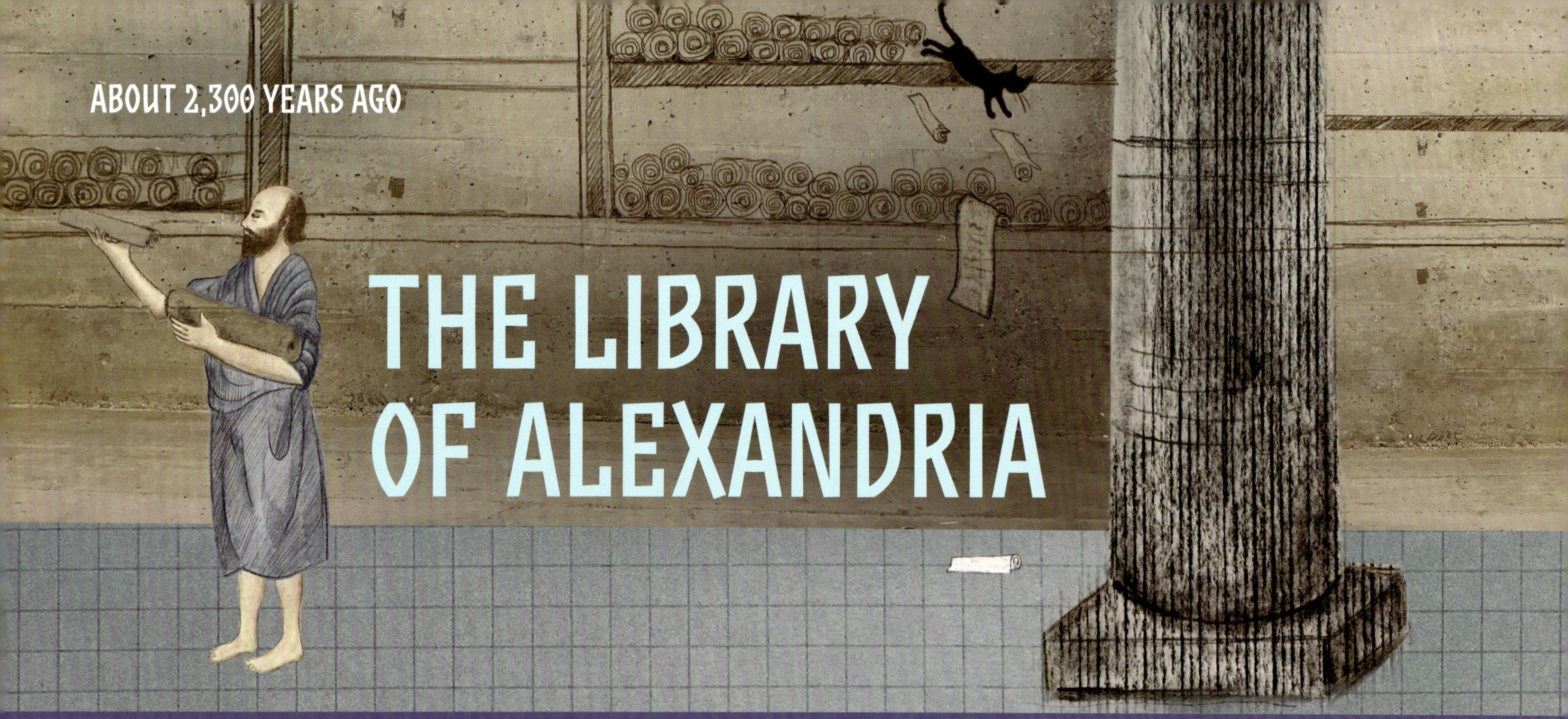

ABOUT 2,300 YEARS AGO

THE LIBRARY OF ALEXANDRIA

As writing developed, the first libraries were built. People wrote down their traditions, stories, and discoveries. These writings needed homes so that more people could come to read them.

The earliest libraries were in Mesopotamia. They held clay tablets with cuneiform writing.

One of the best-known and largest libraries in the ancient world was the Library of Alexandria in Egypt.

The Library of Alexandria held tens of thousands of papyrus scrolls. People traveled long distances to visit it. They read about different cultures. They found out about new discoveries in science and math. It was a place where people from faraway places could come together to learn.

PAGE BY PAGE

▶ **Scribes wrote and drew each page of a book like this by hand. This page tells about a king being crowned.**

For thousands of years, authors wrote on scrolls by hand. Scribes, or people who could write, would make copies by rewriting a text onto new scrolls.

People in Rome made the first books with separate pages. A reader could flip through them to find a particular page.

Scribes in many places continued to copy books by hand. Some of these texts had detailed, colorful art as well as writing. It could take a scribe weeks or months to copy just one book. That made books expensive. A book could cost as much as a house!

◀ **Quill pens were invented more than 1,400 years ago. To write with a quill, a person cut off the end of a bird feather and dipped the cut end into ink.**

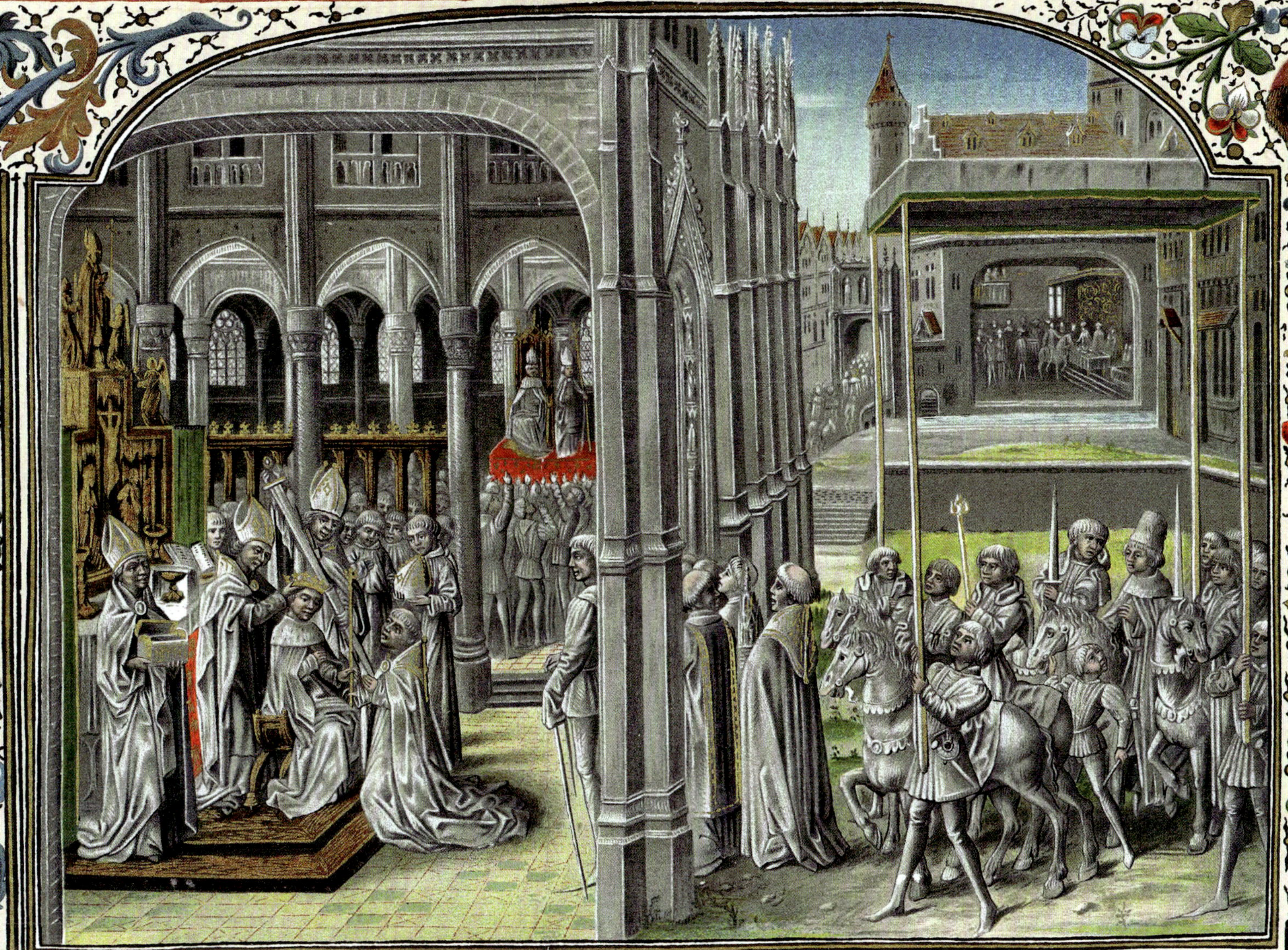

Du couronnement du roy henry / duc de lancastre / Qui se fist du con- sentement de tout le commun dangle terre / Et de la maniere de la feste qui si tint. Le chapitre hxbiij.

En lan de nostre seigneur .mil CCCC. vingt moins / Advint en angleterre ou mois de septembre / et le darrain iour dicellui mois par vng

estoient / Et la fut tout ledit peu- ple assamble a Westmoustier ce mar- dj devant dit / present le duc de lan- castre et ses gens / Et la calenga le duc de lancastre le royaulme dangle terre / et requist a estre roy par trois manieres de cas / Premierement p conquest / Secondement pour tant que il se disoit estre droit hoir de la cou- ronne / Et tierchement par ce que le

ABOUT 1,300 YEARS AGO

BLOCK PRINTING

In China, people invented a new way to make copies of books. It was called block printing.

The Chinese writing system is made up of symbols called characters. Each character stands for a word. To make a block print, a person carved the words for a whole page onto a block of wood. Then they brushed ink over the block and pressed paper onto it to make a print.

If you wanted to make many copies of a page, block printing was faster than writing the words out by hand over and over. But it took a long time to carve each block.

▲ carving words onto a block

▲ using traditional methods to make a block print

MOVABLE TYPE

Block printing was an improvement over writing by hand. Then a Chinese inventor named Bi Sheng created movable type, a quicker way to get pages ready to print.

Bi made clay blocks in the shape of each Chinese character. This was a big job, since there are thousands of characters!

Instead of carving each page, a person could move around the blocks to form a page of text. Wax was used to stick the rows of blocks onto a metal sheet. Then the blocks were covered in ink. Paper was pressed onto them to make a print. Later, people created frames to hold the blocks in place.

▲ This historical drawing shows Bi Sheng making a print with movable type.

▶ Carved blocks could be rearranged to form new sentences.

TRY IT YOURSELF!

MAKE A PRINT

Carve your own letter blocks to stamp out your name!

WHAT YOU NEED

one or more potatoes

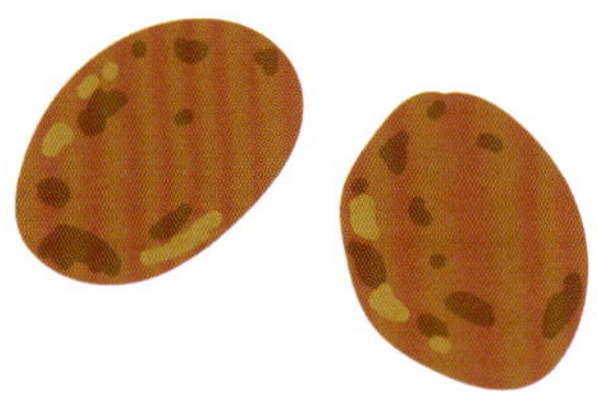

toothpick

plastic knife and spoon

paintbrush

acrylic paint

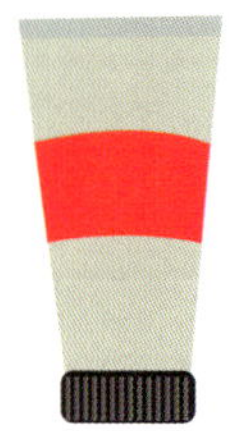

paper

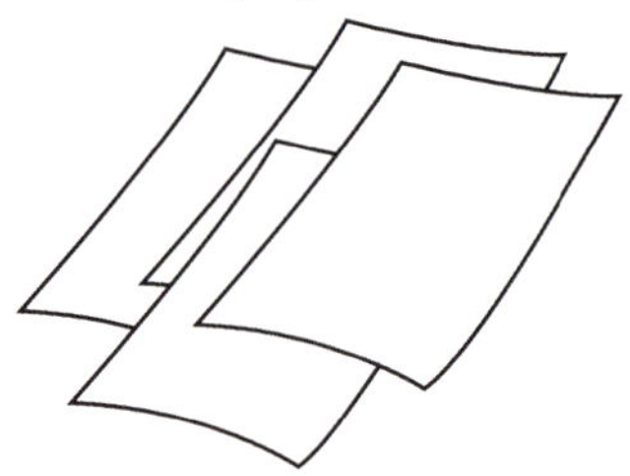

WHAT TO DO

1

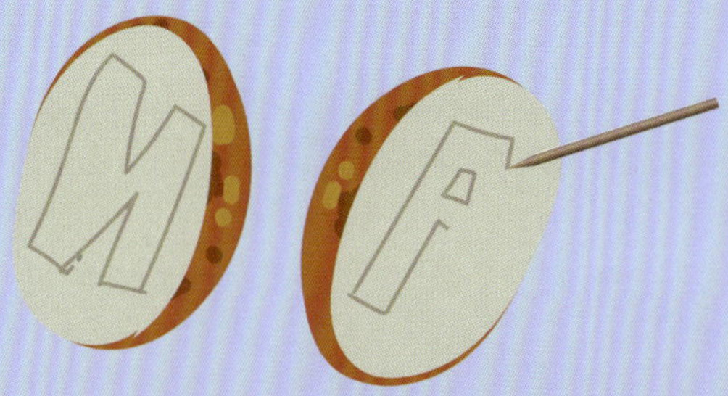

Ask an adult to help you cut a potato in half. On the cut side of each half, mark the outline of a letter with the toothpick. (Hint: Draw each letter backward so it will print forward!)

2

With your plastic knife and spoon, carve and scoop around each outline so a flat letter sticks up.

3

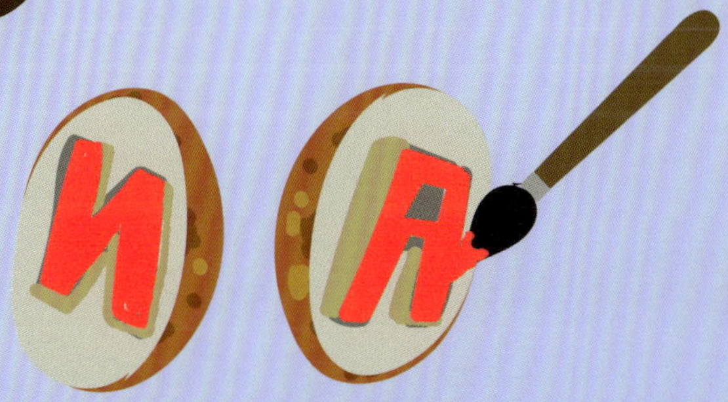

Brush paint onto your potato letter blocks. Press the blocks onto the paper to make a print.

4

Repeat steps 1 to 3 as needed to make more letters and spell out your name. You can use the letter blocks over and over—they will last a few hours.

ABOUT 600 YEARS AGO

THE PRINTING PRESS

▲ **Johannes Gutenberg**

Johannes Gutenberg, a German inventor, created a new machine that could print thousands of pages every day. This machine used Bi Sheng's invention, movable type. Here's how it worked.

1

Workers arranged letter blocks to form words and sentences.

2

They attached the letters to a frame with screws so the blocks wouldn't move. Then the frame was attached to the printing press.

3

Workers covered the blocks with ink. To print a page, they pressed a piece of paper onto the inky blocks.

The printing press printed pages faster than any technology before. A scribe could copy only a few pages a day. A printing press could print thousands of pages a day! And people kept building newer, bigger printing presses that could print even more pages.

SPECIAL DELIVERY

Thanks to the printing press, books could be made by machines. But people kept writing letters by hand to communicate with each other.

Technology played a role in delivering mail. Long ago, it could take weeks for a letter to get to its destination. Take a look to see how new inventions made mail delivery faster over time in the United States.

ABOUT 225 YEARS AGO

STAGECOACHES

Horses pulled heavy carts called stagecoaches. They traveled about as fast as a person running.

ABOUT 200 YEARS AGO

TRAINS

Trains delivered mail faster. But trains must travel on train tracks. This meant trains could deliver letters only between cities where tracks had been built.

ABOUT 120 YEARS AGO TO TODAY

CARS AND TRUCKS

Mail carriers began to use cars, which could reach more places quickly. Mail could be delivered in about half as much time as before.

ABOUT 100 YEARS AGO TO TODAY

AIRPLANES

Airmail, or delivery by plane, became a fast way to send letters across the country. A letter can now often be delivered in just one day.

TRY IT YOURSELF!

MAKE SOME MAIL

Mailing letters was once the quickest way to communicate with someone far away. Have you ever written and mailed a letter? If not, follow these three steps to give it a try!

WHAT TO DO

1 Write your letter.

Write the date you wrote the letter.

Start your letter with the word "Dear." Then write the name of the person you're writing to.

Write your message. It can be as long or as short as you like.

Use a sign-off to end your letter. You can use words like "Sincerely," "From," or "Love."

Write your name at the end of the letter.

September 3, 2025

Dear Grammy,

I just started the second grade! Second grade is different from first grade. I get to try out a lot of new things.

I can read books with chapters now. The librarian even let me take three books home!

We are growing sunflowers in our greenhouse at school. My teacher says they are her favorite flower. They are mine too!

I can't wait to see you soon!

Love,
Luca

2 Address an envelope.

Put your name and address in the top left corner. This way, the letter can be returned to you in case it can't be delivered.

Don't forget a stamp! This sticker is the payment to the post office for delivering your letter.

Write the name and address of the person you are sending your letter to in the middle.

3 Mail your letter.

Put your letter in the envelope, seal it up, and put it in a mailbox. Mail carriers will pick up your letter and deliver it.

DIGITAL TECHNOLOGY

Long ago, it could take weeks to receive a letter. New technologies have made written communication faster and faster.

COMPUTERS

Early computers were the size of a room! Later, computers became smaller and faster. People used them at work, at home, and at school. To share a piece of writing, a person had to print it out or save it onto a small device called a disk.

INTERNET

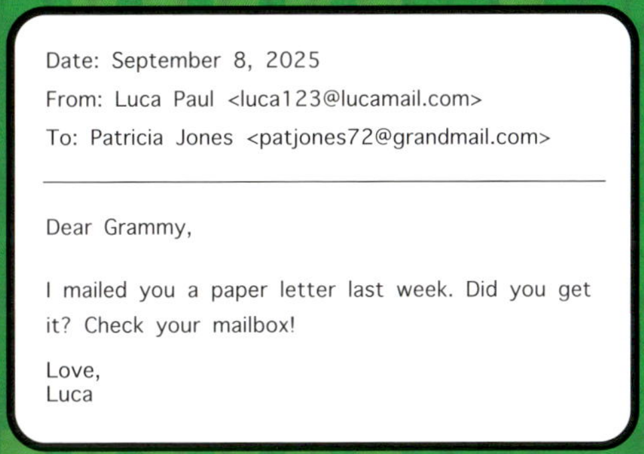

The Internet is a system that connects computers through wires. It made email possible. Someone could write a message on their computer and send it to another computer instantly.

TEXT MESSAGES

Early cell phones had buttons. People pressed the buttons to write text messages and send them to another person's phone. The messages traveled through wireless signals.

SMARTPHONES

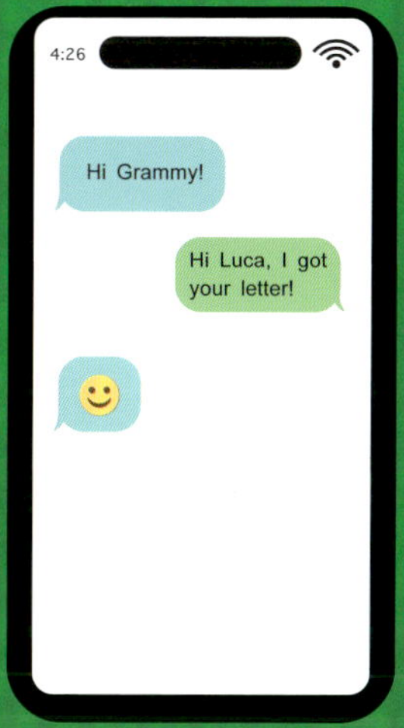

Today, most phones have touch screens you can use to send email and messages, make video calls, play games, and more.

ABOUT 40 YEARS AGO TO TODAY

NEW WRITING SYSTEMS

Technology isn't the only thing changing the way we write. People are still creating new writing systems for languages around the world.

Ibrahima and Abdoulaye Barry are brothers from Guinea, Africa. They are members of the Fulani people. When they were growing up in the 1980s, the Fulani language didn't have its own writing system. People used the Arabic writing system to write Fulani words.

The Arabic alphabet didn't have symbols for some sounds in the Fulani language. That meant some words could not be written clearly with Arabic letters. To solve this problem, the Barry brothers invented an alphabet just for Fulani. They were only ten and fourteen years old when they created it.

The brothers named their alphabet ADLaM. The name comes from the first four letters in the ADLaM alphabet. Since they invented it, many people have learned how to write and read ADLaM. It is taught in schools in several African countries.

Today there is a digital version of ADLaM too. People can use it to write on computers, websites, and cell phones. “ADLaM will help us preserve our culture,” said the Barry brothers.

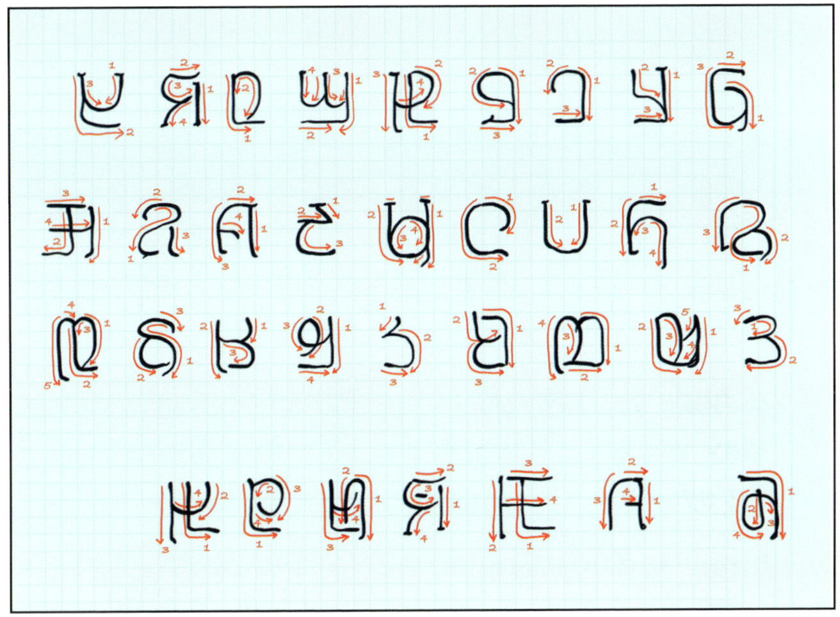

▲ This chart shows how to make capital letters in ADLaM.

▶ The Barry brothers are now adults.

TRY IT YOURSELF!

DESIGN YOUR OWN ALPHABET

The Barry brothers created a new writing system to help people write in a different way. Think about the letters you use in English. How could you design symbols that might help people write in a new way? Follow the steps below to design your own alphabet.

WHAT TO DO

1. Decide how you want your alphabet to help people write differently. Maybe your design has a pattern that new writers can learn more quickly. (Think about letters that you found difficult when you were learning to write.) Or your alphabet might be easier to write if you're left-handed.

2. Write out the letters A to Z. Underneath each letter, write your own symbol. You can also add extra symbols that let a writer express a particular sound or idea. (For example, think about how one little emoji can mean a lot!) On your paper, write what each extra symbol represents.

3. Use your symbols to write a message. Give the message and a copy of your alphabet to a friend, and see if they can decode it!

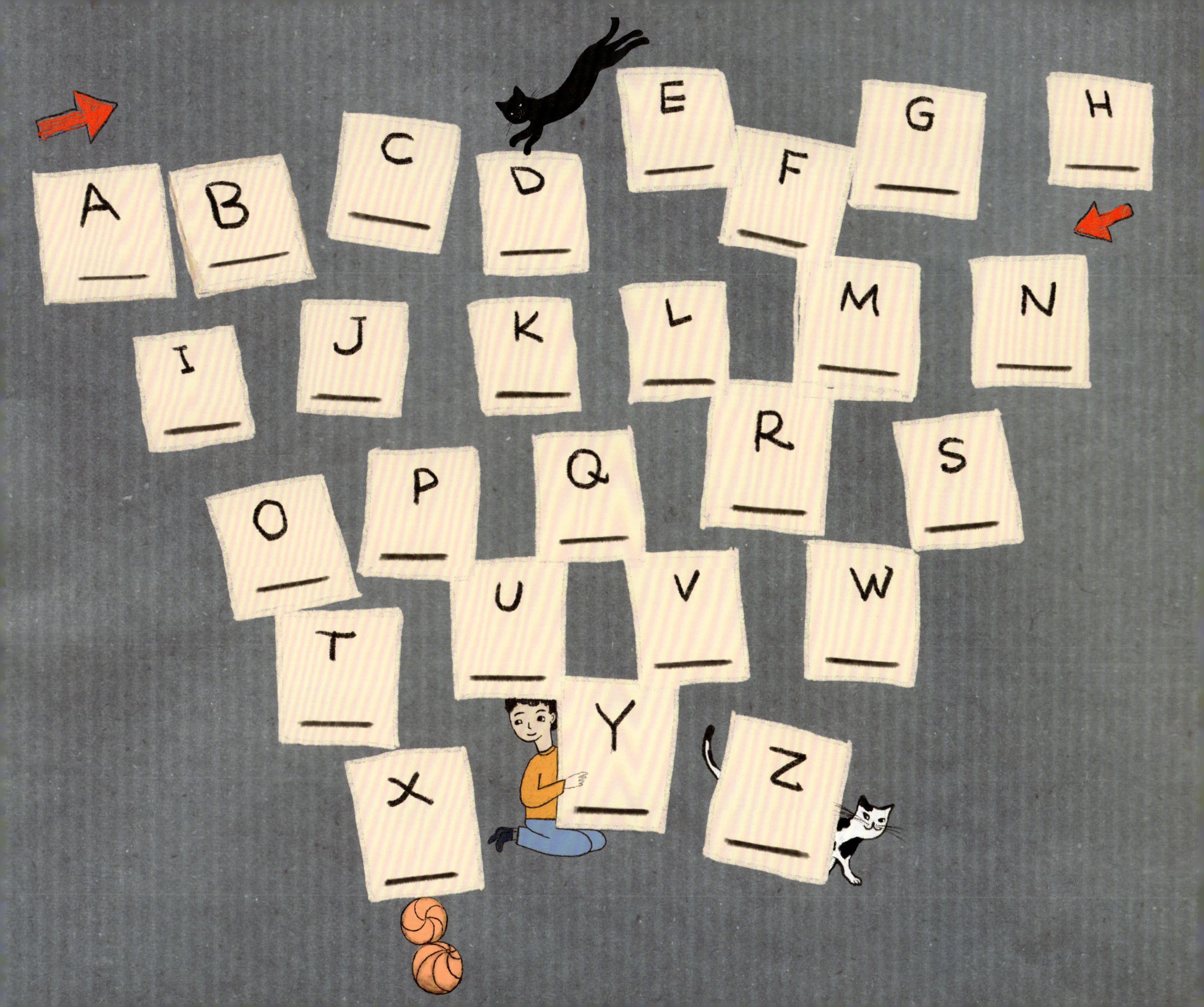
A
B
C
D
E
F
G
H
I
J
K
L
M
N
O
P
Q
R
S
T
U
V
W
X
Y
Z

THE STORY CONTINUES

For thousands of years, people have used writing to share ideas, to learn from one another, to communicate with people far away, and to keep traditions alive. The way we write keeps changing.

We all have a story to tell.

What will your story be?

How will you write it?